THE ROOM IN WHICH I WORK

PREVIOUS WORKS

CHAPBOOKS

Black Anecdote, Poetry Society of America, 2011
NN, Tammy, 2016

The Room In Which I Work

Andrew Seguin

OMNIDAWN PUBLISHING
OAKLAND, CALIFORNIA
2017

Cover Art: Andrew Seguin, Untitled, Cyanotype, 2014
All images in Histories: Andrew Seguin, Untitled Cyanotypes, 2014
All photographs in Les Vendanges are by Andrew Seguin:
p. 72: Saint-Loup-de-Varennes, 2014
p. 73: Rue de l'Oratoire, 2014
p. 74: Le Gras, 2014

Cover and interior typefaces: Adobe Jenson Pro & Perpetua Std
Cover and interior design by Cassandra Smith

Offset printed in the United States
by Edwards Brothers Malloy, Ann Arbor, Michigan
On 55# Glatfelter B18 Antique
Acid Free Archival Quality Recycled Paper

Library of Congress Cataloging-in-Publication Data

Names: Seguin, Andrew, 1981- author.
Title: The room in which I work / Andrew Seguin.
Description: Oakland, California : Omnidawn Publishing, 2017. | Includes
    bibliographical references.
Identifiers: LCCN 2016045486 | ISBN 9781632430359 (pbk. : alk. paper)
Classification: LCC PS3619.E414 A6 2017 | DDC 811/.6--dc23
LC record available at https://lccn.loc.gov/2016045486

Published by Omnidawn Publishing, Oakland, California
www.omnidawn.com   (510) 237-5472   (800) 792-4957
10 9 8 7 6 5 4 3 2 1
ISBN: 978-1-63243-035-9

CONTENTS

I: Can we talk a little about your vocabulary

NN: You mean words

I: Words—you never used just one to describe the camera

NN: What's a camera

I: Right, the apparatus or box you were using, once technicians and history had their way with it, it came to be called camera in English or *appareil photo* in French

NN: So I wasn't too far off. But my use of *helio* didn't last then

I: No they took the sun out of it

NN: Hard to do

I: Ha, yes, but we say *photographie*, photographer, *photographique, photomaton,* photo booth, photochemical, photo finish, photo lab, photo sensitive, family photo, passport photo

NN: I see the reference to writing is often lost

I: True

NN: Light is the most important part of the word

HISTORIES

Authority loves fixed points, so it is commonly written that the birth of photography occurred in 1839. It is in January of that year that Louis Jacques-Mandé Daguerre, a Parisian painter and set designer noted for his Diorama—a theater in which large painted tableaux reveal illusions and change color and atmosphere through the manipulation of light—first displays to the French Académie des Sciences his *daguerréotype*, a photographic process that produces a positive image of uncanny clarity on a mirrored, metal surface. After learning of Daguerre's announcement, William Henry Fox Talbot, an Englishman who, since 1834, has been conducting photographic research and trying to record images from a camera obscura, hastens to show to the Royal Society his own process, which he calls "photogenic drawing," and from which he will later develop both negative and positive images. But the principles of photography—light's behavior when passing through an aperture, the photosensitivity of certain chemicals, the need to arrest that sensitivity—had been known since the early 18th century. By 1839 an uncertain number of photographic images had already been made. In the 1790s, Thomas Wedgwood, son of the English ceramicist Josiah Wedgwood, uses silver to make several photograms which, being unfixed, fade back into darkness, and occasionally surface as rumors in the present tense. And by 1833, Nicéphore Niépce, who was once Daguerre's partner, is dead. It is Niépce who, in 1826 or 1827, takes what is considered to be the first known photograph from nature, through a method he calls *heliographie*. To be clear: he inserts a light-sensitized pewter plate inside a modified camera obscura, points it out a window of his home, and makes a photograph of the surrounding roofs and a distant pear tree.

I carry a camera, which is to say I carry a question: what should I photograph? Why should I photograph? For many years I never thought this way. I took pictures.

*

It is 1812. Russia hisses away from Napoleon like a fuse, and in Germany the Brothers Grimm publish a collection of tales, which includes the story of a man who learns the languages of dogs, frogs and doves. In the Burgundy region of France, Nicéphore Niépce is searching for stones. There is no such thing as photography.

*

More and more I lift the camera to compose a photograph, my eye flitting through the viewfinder like a dragonfly to find the proper framing, the angle that changes a morsel of the world into a compelling picture, but I do not release the shutter. I am often not able to stand where I want to stand because of traffic patterns, street width, or other circumstances of space, but more often I feel the resulting photograph would have no value, a judgment only the camera can help me to make.

*

The 18th century is turning into the 19th, the ideas associated with photography are floating across continents—does one refuse to light amongst the short-lived clouds of fireflies, or are they all walking back to their studies, saying it smells like rain?

*

"The animals of the mind cannot be so easily dispersed."

– John Berger

*

Atop Nicéphore's cane, a dog's head, carved from bone.

Nicéphore, from the Greek Nikephoros, "one who carries victory." Listed on his baptismal certificate: Joseph Niépce. Carved on his tomb: M. Joseph Nicephore Niepce as well as Nicephore Niepce, the latter added in 1933. Carved on the plaque on the house where he was born: Nicephore Niepce. On the monument behind Le Gras: J. Niceph.re Niepce, the "re" rendered like an exponent. On the one along route 906: Nicephore Niepce. How he signed his letters: J.N. Niépce. How I hear, write and say his name: Nicéphore Niépce.

*

To speak of it, he had to speak of how to speak of it. He spoke of "objects painting themselves," "the possibility of painting in this way," "copying views from Nature," "fixing objects received in the camera obscura."

*

Nikon FG
Holga
Mamiya 645
Nikon N90
Diana
Harinezumi
Hasselblad 503C
Lumix
A pinhole I built of plywood

*

30.5 cm tall, 31.5 cm wide, and 37 cm long when closed. The dimensions of Niépce's sliding box camera.

*

"Photography is commonly regarded as an instrument for knowing things."

– Susan Sontag

*

I am right-handed but hold the camera to my left eye.

Niépce applies the term *heliographie* to two distinct processes: reproducing, by photographic means, existing images of engravings; and enabling, or allowing, an image of the landscape to paint itself on metal inside a camera obscura.

*

Silver nitrate suspended in chalk, the suspension poured into a jar, the jar wrapped with a paper stencil of words, the words blackening in the sun, the paper removed to show the words floating there so strangely that "many who were curious about the experiment but ignorant of its nature took occasion to attribute the thing to some sort of trick," Johann Heinrich Schulze, 1717.

*

"Across what distances in time do the elective affinities and correspondences connect? How is it that one perceives oneself in another human being, or if not oneself, one's own precursor?"

—W.G. Sebald

*

Camera as *mezzaluna*, mincing time. Time in which I've come to doubt the camera as an instrument that can bestow value, value being the shadow on the far side of the question I was asked: "How do you decide to take a picture?" Pictures I've taken of bus schedules, maps, addresses—opening the shutter being faster than writing.

*

Writing in French in Brazil, the inventor Hercules Florence uses the verb *photographier* in 1834. In February 1839, variations on the term appear independently in English, French and German. (Geoffrey Batchen)

*

Niépce's other research, often carried out with his brother: up the Saône we go by motor; take we water from the Seine to Versailles; can we grow woad around the Continental Blockade; dear cousin, we've refined beet sugar.

Niépce marries Agnés Romero in Nice the same week that Robespierre is beheaded.

*

As a ladder transverses space by being mostly space, the photograph transverses time.

*

"In other words, *graphy* can be read as either active or passive (either and therefore never simply one or the other). Operating simultaneously as verb and noun, this writing produces while being produced, inscribes even as it is inscribed."

– Geoffrey Batchen

*

On trains to Burgundy I often heard the line *Dis, Blaise, sommes-nous bien loin de Montmartre?* and I thought yes, we are far from Montmartre, and we are farther from other times than we are from other places, we no longer bike home from work to change and rush to the darkroom on Monday nights. *Dis, c'était comment de travailler dans la chambre noire?* It was to leave behind, by means of a revolving door, the sun, and the fluorescent-yellow light of the deadline, and to enter a blood-colored light, that of the safelight, under which I felt my main object was to evaluate black, the vocabulary of black, for in photographic paper black has a weight and depth and gloss entirely unto itself, a dimension that seems to proffer entrance to some original source, although it is of course a surface, so I made test strip after test strip to decide—and here you might hear the repeated, creaking triangle of the paper cutter—how the black should speak, which is to say how the black should look, and through its posture encourage all the other values in the photograph, like the instrument in an orchestra to which all other instruments tune, for in that room black was not the color of endings the night suggests as it falls, but the matter in which all looking occurs.

*

The average human hand cannot hold a camera steady enough to prevent image blur at speeds slower than $1/30^{th}$ of a second. The less breath in the body, the less average the hand.

Upon first seeing his portrait, I felt he might use a file for a comb.

*

It cannot be corroborated, the story that Nicéphore earned demerits at the Oratory for organizing, after the priests had gone to bed, projections of the magic lantern.

*

As years pass images accrete, and it feels more and more difficult to summon the boy in the darkroom who watches through the developer a birdfeeder emerge from a blank piece of paper.

*

"Nostalgia is memory decayed to sugar, she thought on a bench in the plaza of a massive glass box."

— Donna Stonecipher

*

Has every picture since smeared novocaine on the first?

*

According to one study, 17 seconds is the average length of time a visitor to a museum spends looking at a work of art.

*

Sent by stagecoach to his brother Claude in January 1817, a basket containing

Two crocks of jam
One head cheese
Two fat hens
61 bottles of wine — 15 from Jambles, 46 from Mellecey

*

To measure the percentage of life that occurs at "eye-level:"

Camera as adding machine, issuing receipts. Camera as framing device. Camera as recording device. Camera as sketchbook (Henri Cartier-Bresson). Camera as "box of air" (Christopher James). Camera as object of suspicion. Camera as something I still believe in, although more and more I make cameraless photographs, no machine between me and the light.

*

Niépce and Agnés had three children together, two of whom they lost: Claude at the age of 2 and a half in 1800, and Amédée at the age of 6 in 1807. Isidore, their eldest son, who was born in 1795, lived long enough to receive, as a gift for his daughter, a package of dresses from Louis Daguerre.

*

I often forget it is silent, the sun.

*

"For me the noise of Time is not sad: I love bells, clocks, watches—and I recall that at first photographic implements were related to techniques of cabinetmaking and the machinery of precision: cameras, in short, were clocks for seeing, and perhaps in me someone very old still hears in the photographic mechanism the living sound of the wood."

– Roland Barthes

*

It is from Niépce's lensmaker, an optician in Paris, Vincent Chevalier, that Daguerre learns of his heliographic research.

*

Partial list of materials, compiled by Niépce and Daguerre:

Lavender oil
White petroleum
Alcohol
Copal
Camphor
Water
Bitumen of Judea
Daylight
Mastic
Pewter
White asphalt
Polished silver
Virgin leather
Iodine
White glass
Black glass
Heat
Thunderstorm
Humidity
Time
Light
Volatility
Sulfuric acid
Kid-skin dabbers
Resin
Varnish
Nature
Phosphor
Table salt
Emptiness

*

Sun bears down on the tops of clouds so the day is overcast but bright, and I
set out to take pictures. On my light meter I dial in the ASA of the film (400),
the aperture I want to use (f22) on my camera, then I hold the light meter up
to a docked boat, and read it. I read the value of the light falling on the hull,
or I read the value of the light reflecting off of it. In either case, because of the
photographic properties—light, aperture, shutter and film speed—that converge
when the meter's white carbuncle becomes literate, I can reliably predict how

the tonal value of that boat will appear on the negative, or I can manipulate that value by changing one or more of the three variables that I am able to change. Two of my cameras look at this reliability askance, literally, for their lenses do not record what I see through their viewfinders, only approximations. A third has no viewfinder, and is just a box I must try to place on the right planes.

*

Because of weak vision, in 1826 Niépce purchased spectacles with blue-tinted lenses.

*

In summer we slept with the windows open, and in the middle of the night my father could hear, coming from the boarding house next door, the sound of typing. It was the sound of one of our neighbors, Nancy. "I write plays," she told my father when he asked. Besides writing plays, Nancy cared for Frances, the one-legged owner of the boarding house, for whom there was a ramp leading up to the side entrance, which was visible from our kitchen and bathroom, and from the stained glass window on the landing of our stairwell, when I cared to look out at the world in diamonds of cobalt, mustard and rust. When Frances died, she bequeathed the house—a beautiful but run-down red brick Victorian—to Nancy. Nancy asked my father to make a video of the interior, not to help her with selling the property, but to be another form of memory for her, a record of the years she had passed there. My father agreed, mainly because he had always wanted to see the interior of that house, and he and a cameraman spent a day with Nancy in its dark wooden rooms, and what he remembers most is that it had a 30-foot long white porcelain sink, like a trough. What I remember most is how that house felt impassable. Although Nancy had just inherited the house, she had no money. As payment for the video she offered my father a Nikon FG, a manual 35mm camera, still in its box, which she had never used. He in turn offered it to me for my 12th birthday, judging correctly that I would be interested in photography. I do not know for how many years that camera slept next door to me, waiting for me to open its eye. I do know the first things I photographed were robins, cardinals and squirrels.

*

Facts sound like facts, while speculation creates an uneven percussion: Joseph Nicéphore Niépce was born in Chalon-sur-Saône, France, on March 7, 1765, and died in Saint-Loup-de-Varennes, France, on July 5, 1833. Of light brown hair. Grey eyes. A wide forehead. Among his concerns were debt, building a combustion motor with his brother Claude, the harm done to crops by frost, and a method of writing with the sun.

WINTER

I: You once put a stone in your device

NN: I studied lithography so quarried some stone, stone veined red I varnished that it might be changed by the light

I: Changed

NN: So the order of light and shadow inverts, the dark looks white, the white dark

I: And you had that idea by looking through your box

NN: I had the dovecote, barn and pear tree upside down and shrunk, as if I looked from another side of my eye

I: Would you say you wanted to get to that other side

NN: Are there debts there?

I: Ha. So what was the varnish made of

NN: We should move on

TUESDAY: HISTORY OF PHOTOGRAPHY

Twice the scent of skunk made an arrest:
I paused but saw nothing in the gloss

of leaf mass, nothing but ballerinas
being corrected in a window further

in the chronic rain. Sulfur and a rose
blur of forms become my instructor,

Joseph, but it is grey. I sniff the city
for a picture, although my blood

feels done with silver, mind weary
of providing for the future another

frame. And yet it's almost mystery
how the machines frequent my eye,

that they might splice it right again
by destroying old leases on space.

It is winter where you were born
and the rain is recording my work.

My camera listens for the sun in woodsmoke
and potted cyclamen, its mirror not even

breathing in the dark. Dark chamber,
dark room, room of shadows, wooden box.

FEBRUARY, JAMBLES

Vines stitch the hills
to seal the earth

from snow that stayed
a thought all winter,

and birds are suspicious
it's spring: the sun,

consecutive. A dog next
to a just pink dogwood

barks: he too smells
a future in the cedars:

the light will be soiled
tomorrow and I will not

work. That I lived in a
desert and made no visits.

That I engraved a ghost me
to see to the guests.

The time I have I pass,
fashioning another eye.

THE WEATHER, DEAR COUSIN

Go the two seasons
on different principles:
green house, white horse.

In the first I work
the hours' lamps empty.
The second I am taken

off hoof by hoof
beyond all hope of
shadows pinned to stone.

It is the snow-prints
I would mimic, but they hide
from the sun and last

just long enough to
show how to be gone.

MULHOUSE

In Alsace at night I smelled a horse
which made a picture: walnut head
behind a fence, body next like

a worked-out zeppelin, black tail
that twitched half a serif, some
calligraphy. There a picture

because pictures conditioned me:
I was a sonogrammed pumpkin seed;
as I grew so did the records

of being, asleep, at bat, alert
watching orange bobbers on a pond,
of late an aging face that betrays

no acknowledgment its eyes advance
through streets as if rectangles
are the shapes to see, as if what's made

to feel falls at cinema's ratio,
and all hope for a developed self derives
from repeated poses of auto-portraiture.

She was borderless, this horse.
She occurred in the dark like a passing
conversation about parabolas.

It was then I remembered the camera
that resembled furniture, replete
with fine joinery I admired as I admire

barns in post-and-beam. Inside its single
hole was night, perpetual, vast like a season
but also smaller, denser, like a hinge.

À PROPOS THE MOTOR, 1817

      From town I had sent
      something very black:

solid asphalt
called *Bitumen of Judea*

      which I pulverized
      and burned

with charcoal
I found in the bedroom of the gardener

      —helped the candle up the wall

I: You had some success with glass

NN: Yes, in 1822 I gave my cousin the General an image of Pope Pius VII I had copied from an engraving

I: I read that he

NN: Hauled it all over France until it was shattered by some maladroit's hand?

I: Yes, and he gave you back the empty frame

NN: Gold-plated copper, the better to hold the air

HE WAS JOSEPH, FIRST

Noon sounds like the cathedral bells
push the river through winter,
the water's surface such a surface
that it's not a color. Roman ruins,
old roses, I can't bend enough

for a better angle. Haven't I
come to take a picture, its plural?
Thought a moment was coming when
sun would cut the wool from afternoon;
no. On to who-you-are duty.

I can feel near futures in which I'll be
asked my impressions of a city
that's as much shutters as it is windows,
some shut houses touched in Southern
colors, the water ones, where one

could say such a shade of yellow
thought better of appearing
so bright. It's grey—
the house of the man whose hours
were asphalt, lavender and tin.

SPRING

NO MORE FILM

Azaleas and chain grease,
almost April. On the train
the landscape asked "Will you
say of me you know my stone?"
Warmer month, greener river,

swan feet kicking orange peels
beneath the water, long
exposure. The first tourist boat
tied up like a block of ice.
Theory. a tree is a picture

of the history of spring.
Its flowers carry past tense
into the currents of continuous
present: branches bloomed,
we say "the tree is blooming."

YOUR PACKET, DEAR COUSIN

Into my snuffbox the excellent
tobacco you sent
           arrived perfectly.

Same cannot be said for the
carriage lantern;
           its double curve

darkens its function past
correction.
           Woad and beet sugar

eat into what I would
devote to my
           machines:

with regret I watch the most
beautiful season
           of the year unfold

no results. I have no guide but
imagination: the cotton
           has not yet come in.

ALBEDO

Roofs with a populace
of moss, moss burned for fuel

in the land before images
were things to which we compared

the world. The world: indigo, God
and wine plots, spring river rising

the debts rising too. Claude's garden
blooms and the butcher's buying wine.

"To paint itself"—a verb
you left outside all afternoon.

THE EXPERIMENTS — TO CLAUDE, 1817

Days all I am
        are obstacles, not a color
        on the stone in the *obscure*

despite the light, immediate
and resin spread thin with thanks
                to caloric acid

as you know no more silver muriate
        but more and more me, a sentry
        for what alcohol attacks

or leaves harden in the sun
as you know not
        your oldest cow has a cough

"MY HELIOGRAPHIC WORK IS IN FULL SWING"

Donkey sun, shoulders
of coal and pollen, *despite*

your excellence the experiment failed,

tin scrap scratching gravel
like an animal. Blossoms dare

the frost, *a net to catch the thrush*

who sings for us Is there incense
to this picture, what is this picture

of? Towards Autun to look up

stone, *I broke my lens of sharpest focus.*
Off went the crow who had ended

the sentence of the power lines.

Rain exceeds its noun by falling everywhere and not always visibly. 1816, Niépce attempted to capture on paper an image from a modified camera obscura, an image that, due to the optical properties of light rays herded through an aperture (note: in the wet ash of February he appeared to me a shepherd for these strange worms), showed the dovecote of his property, Le Gras, upside down and in reverse.

Rain, Chalon-sur-Saône, for weeks I lived on the family tree of these sounds. Fields mentioned in Niépce's letters looked like sump; like him I creased the edges of paper in waiting for better weather (note: at its origin, photography is like agriculture—dependent on the sun). And with the sun of May Niépce succeeded in capturing two images on paper, or so he writes in sending the examples to his brother Claude, examples perhaps showing the now-vanished dovecote and the now-gone neighboring buildings, the roof and chimney of the bakehouse, a likely mass of black lace: the pear tree.

Other species have replaced the air there after more than a century: speculation, sycamores cast in their usual role of facts showing bone, suited to the dog barks that circled the property as I did, looking for a way in, a view past. Nicéphore does not describe in this letter what his brother should see (note: one of humanity's oldest activities) and turns his words to the recent armor on the vines—hoarfrost of no consequence—the beauty of the fava beans, and a lately, gentle rain.

THE EXPERIMENTS – SPRING 1817

This, my hand, burned foreign
      by phosphor
      I give now to gummish

materials—resin of gaïac
which reddish clings to stone

And move in no way
      like a giant: call him happy
      who engraves a lily

HE'S OUT _____ PICTURES

Earlier and earlier daylight authorized me to wake
lit the stripe on the ring-necked pigeon as if to light it by name
after first anointing the cat with its forehead

With one camera loaded and one camera charged
I left the third closed like Sunday in its bag
which didn't change the fact sun plus a mirror makes a factory

From the latticework, brandished lilacs
carp in the park pond moved East like stitches
joining the surface to the depth

But I wasn't ready for such an idea
as two days ago when the rainbow felt forged
by gods playing horseshoes—the camera was at home

And clouds held the sky to a blue rule of thirds
wind wanted to rinse my mouth with dust
and reposition a family's snapshot

A desert fog coming off the gravel adding portent
to their new silhouettes, describing them as barely
there—if this were sixty years ago "barely there"

Might come home as memory with a scalloped edge
as it is I came home having taken no pictures
except the one they asked me to take

MONT AVRIL

Foreground, grasshopper; background,
Chalon. To the mountain I bring
my vocabulary. The way is daisies,

something-cups and a low yellow
species whose suffix is -bells.
Shin chiseled by stalks of wild raspberry.

I walk to see the vista, the view, the outlook,
the distance, the one of many points
of interest. Sandwich at the panorama,

insect quick to sugar on my finger.
Hundred years of thunder and the cross
has lost your name. An alphabet of lichen

covers what might have been the double
clunk of Ns. My thumb is blind.
Nothing on the stone rhymes with phosphor.

I: Some say it was the motor that was your true work

NN: It's a funny word, we took a boat up the Saône against the current, true

I: But it never caught on, never brought you the money you hoped

NN: No, Claude never did much with it in England, it never advanced, never sold

I: Although a material you initially tried for the motor's propulsion—*Bitumen of Judea*—ended up stopping time

NN: The Egyptians used it for mummies

NEAR FUTURE

In April walls grow hair again
and some purple mops the gravel

when a finger points
to the source of the year turning over

The sun, old sea creature
suctions us predictable on the quays

all afternoon who help the hours
brush themselves of turnips

and the names that snow unscrolled
(no one writes prepositions in a field)

My teeth stamp the thesis
that, for now, the future is getting longer

Overheard: a cloud of preludes to bed
one argument for free will, clear video

and a kid dug a coin out of the grout
A fair price, these flowers for winter

SUMMER

TO CLAUDE

Came a man whose business
is Swiss cows. Came clouds
of gunpowder to interrupt

my work, even though I've learned
the box needs no sun
to function. I built a third

one. And in cardboard
hemmed my lens a new aperture,
but know not the right ratio,

nor what will come of this gas
I pipe in the device, if any will
burn an image in stone. I send

you your bellows in a pine box
Baptiste made, its empty space
packed by my wife with bruised pears.

ANNIVERSARY

Is this age: days akin to waste
rack up efficacy, are so

deft at being gone
I never think to believe

they might have been engraved;
through the open window

comes a wiffle ball
like a hieroglyph,

a handshake is the signal
for the guests to begin

forgetting my name;
there is cold onyx

in my glass to keep the whiskey whole;
I can feel my hair is public

but my scalp is personal;
the slide is a y-axis

where children mock the body's
decline, all evening creak and glee

will there be another ping
to announce coming events

the way the host's oven timer
alerts the fray to chow;

a squirt of gritty soap to cut
the hands' activity

they remember neither
first bones nor berry stains;

I am late to the table
because I cannot count

the purple martins in their home,
just black holes;

is this worth a name:
walls trod

by paintings of buffalo
while the chandelier's ochre

sprays encouragement;
watch, the dish is hot;

rosemary that's for memory
the fifth taste, for dark

CUT LIST

Now that I've set to
    building it
finitude   has set in

(at every castle: dandelions
    in the kill slots)
the taffy of months   touched in

January pulled apart
    in chestnut pollen
and strawberries   (tell the kings

I am sick of their ornament)
    As the sun sets at bedtime
I repeat my   measurements

and the new word
    for plywood: *contreplaqué*
which my tongue   sands around

my mouth as I account
    for the matter lost to saw
blades   (millimeters; the palace

statues have lost hands)
    and calculate my cut
list, first in   pencil then in pen

And sketch my camera
    that will have no
mirror nor   meter nor lens

just a hole whose focus
    is infinite, the distance
that is also   a substance

And for which I have never
    built a house but this house
I will begin   with glue

I: The *point de vue d'après nature*, which you made on pewter at Le Gras in the summer of 1826 or 1827, is now considered to be the first fixed photograph from a camera

NN: I had made others by that point

I: I know but they vanished

NN: In the light

I: Or in time

NN: But you have this one

I: The University of Texas has it

NN: I never went to Texas

I: No you went to England and took the plate there, or had it sent, to show Frances Bauer, and eventually he died and it was passed on and put in a box in someone's attic

NN: Finally someone found it

I: Exactly

NN: I imagine it's one of the views from my window

I: Showing the dovecote and the roof of the bakehouse and the *beurré-blanc* pear tree

NN: *Beurré-blanc*! So you've seen it

I: Both the *point de vue* and the view from that window

NN: What have they done to my house

MEDITATION ON AN ALBUM

Pictures, please
　　stop conjugating
my family

I have seen
　　when you cannot
slow down stars

And their light
　　trails off record
to the well

Nor every summer
　　do you catch trees
putting shadows in their pockets

Before night swipes
　　them back and teaches
how to turn a bruise into tar

I do, but I do
　　not catch much
anymore, just watch

After 33 years
　　of 36 exposures I try to
watch what addition I can

Without suggesting
　　with leather we bind
the evidence

Of all occurring faces
　　and force gladness
onto past declensions

In so many houses
　　the living rooms
go on living

With a yellow
   assembly of people
who are not

And it smells of olives
   to remember
And it feels of wood gloss on the palm

And in the picture
   they speak again
but the neighborhood is gone

Like a raccoon
   caught reaching for a bauble
time has chewed off its paw

Hobbled off and left
   the recordings
in the trap

Which I cannot rinse
   of *is* nor the nouns
Father, Mother, Son

In the mouth
   of the river Continuous
whose waters best accept

Parts of speech
   with shallow draft
like the verb *to let*

To let a room
   let fly, to let
go, to let me

Let my life
   wreck and float
on all its tenses

TO CLAUDE, 1824

Since your letter of Sunday last
         grief first found ink

We repeat the King
is dead, long live

                    as I thought: acid did not
attack enough the landscape

which setback I can explain
         only by divulging what's best kept quiet

"I'VE DECIDED TO CARRY OUT
THE EXPERIMENT AT A LARGER SCALE"

An accident of dusk, my bike lock
was struck like a tuning fork
and the rose turned over its duty

of blooms to the moonflower.
My camera slowed its breath to half
a second of exposure

but left me to remember the shine
of limestone as it volleyed back
the sound of wheels on gravel, a tennis

it's played for centuries. In 1838,
Louis Daguerre's first image of living persons
showed living included receiving

a shoe shine on an empty boulevard.
Living still can, and fluorescents
warbling out, safety gates snapping down

to seal off with rubber the hours
of commerce from the hours of mind
drawing a rhombus between

the weedy flowers on which it rests.
At these times of day light
anoints even the least objects—

mulch chips, a blown-off circular
of coupons—with a presence, their forms
seeming the perfect fulfillment

of the circumstance of existence.
Nicéphore Niépce made no images of living persons
and was not among them by July 5, 1833.

Niépce made copies of engravings
and pictures of landscapes, calling these latter
points de vue, indicating the importance

of where one stands.
He stood at the window
of the room in which he worked,

in a house in Saint-Loup-de-Varennes,
Burgundy, France, a house to which I biked
in late winter when wheels sounded out

the hiss of mud and nothing but the river
bloomed. On that ride the landscape
blurred and halted in keeping with my speed

towards the location where the first
known photograph was made, and I wondered
which farmhouse's grout had fallen under

Niépce's gaze, and if in these fields
his pigeons glutted on grain.
Records expire, the dairy cow chews

indifferently, and the sun in which
events occurred remains more or less the same,
minus greater deflections of atmosphere,

and later persons continue looking behind them
for some form of completion,
some dredged feeling to nod at life's trajectory

as simply as the rhododendron does,
filling out with spike and pink the hour
between the dog and the wolf.

As a living person, Niépce rode a kind
of bike, a *draisienne*, known in English
as a dandy horse, a wooden cycle

without pedals that must be fueled
by the rider's pushing, and for which
we remember him building an adjustable seat.

THE EXPERIMENTS

I coated paper with brothers
to the sun, rust and saffron;
I gassed them; I watched until

all I'd done had gone jonquil;
I changed my mind to oxygen;
I invited acids and switched

paper for stone, but stone
stayed its way for centuries,
opaque; the luminous fluid

would stain nothing, nothing
besides my wonder at what it is
to be at once everywhere, and fugitive.

CAMERA OBSCURA

In the annals
I will add to the good omen of the beetle
a thunderstorm on a birthday.
Lightning cleans light
    for the clearing when the *camera obscura*

        inhales again through its aperture
        the visible

on the other side of its hole. And lights
        its interior. And inverts
the image like the human eye,
my model
        without a mirror to perform the wonder of the brain

                so the mansards
           remain upside down on the back wall

of the box,
their reflected light
        rays descending and crossing
              the rays from succulents—
        green things evolved in a symmetry
        that a changed direction
does not disturb—

which rise up.
In the year 1028 in Cairo

        the mathematician Ibn al-Haytham
        began his *Book of Optics*
which describes these principles
and a device that
        Johannes Kepler in 1604 built and called *camera obscura*

and which Nicéphore Niépce
was modifying in 1816

in order to fix these principles
as an image,
what we would call
a photograph
landscape with parameters
fingernail of time

(say *crop, rotate, enlarge*
you speak in the shadow of a display case
for natural laws)

although they can't be but trashed
most of this year's moments
the portrait of a thunderhead resembles
a president
and for centuries the eye
has never been the same
it knows well what it does
camera, blinking kin

Do you believe the thing possible?
Louis Daguerre wrote to Niépce
and it was
possible—some think Niépce may have thought it
so
since a trip to Sardinia
confluence of sun
and Army cartographers

projecting coordinates in the *chambre obscure*
over an island of known silver mines

(Solinus: "*India ebore, argento Sardinia, Attica melle*")

Possible. Speculation sticks up its hair
and history—*happened*—swallows its materials
(try to keep a dog from water)
although lately we are better
at making old throats spit up
blood aurochs
blown on the wall of a cave

A year older
Paris occurs at least twice on my balcony

Of Niépce I read entries on bitumen (*Devil's shit*)
                silver salt white petroleum iodine copper
                        lavender mercury tin and various
oils including Dippel's and that of animals

Other traps for animals were pits
        dug and covered
        with leaves
                        for the bear to fall into
                and in the photograph from which I learned that
the bear is a lighter black than its hole

LES VENDANGES

SHORT BIOGRAPHIES

1. On the 4th of July, 1833, you declined to see Robert the Devil at the theater. On the 5th you were dead.

2. God cut loose the wolf's leg muscle and threw it in the grass; arose the snake. God used his nails to scrape a stripe in the ground East of home, into which he poured silver; arose the Saône. God wrote to you on your fiftieth birthday with the first letter of the world: it was the sun.

3. Resin, stone, gas, petroleum, lavender, phosphor, moss, squash—from each he asked a secret.

4. As children, with canines and knife, you and your brother Claude whittled wheeled machines from wood, whose parts moved like electrical current.

5. Grandfather's microscope lens fit to a box—we call this a camera.

6. "M. Niépce once sent us a stone. M. Niépce once sent us woad. Now he sends us smoke." – The Government

7. In 1798 in Nice, he was kept without a new passport by bureaucrats, after a long voyage to Sardinia was interrupted by uprising in Genoa, sea storms and sickness on the Mediterranean, not to mention five days of hiding out beneath a lighthouse to avoid the hounding of a British corsair, which had arrived to attack in the night. Between the horizon and a ferry boat, it is believed, he first had an idea about photography.

8. In a dream a boar gouged a hole in the bedroom, and he woke inside a camera.

9. "He was not a genius of the first order." – Fouque

10. The lease was up on the bar of your name.

11. Light and shadow he understood as optical phenomena as well as illusions; if their order could be reversed, then so, too, could the world.

12. Inside a box and upside down danced a pear tree. Heliography harvested this anomaly.

13. "For weeks I have made nothing but war against the countryside." – Niépce

14. In 1816, inside a camera obscura, Niépce captured a negative image on silver-soaked paper. Over the next ten years he focused on how he could make prints from such an image, or produce a positive and make it clearer, as well as stable, that it might sustain itself in the light.

15. "Any news of Daguerre? Is he on his way back from the Black Forest?"
    – Niépce

16. He chose neither priest nor lawyer.

LAST VISIT TO CHALON

Tree through the bow
    of a ship
run aground.

    Where the channel
shallows out
    and the church

shadow's cut in half.
    Toward the bridge
with ox eyes to let high water

    through. Stones I'd crossed
but never seen. Swans
    in the mosquitoes' crib,

heron like a sink pipe
    come alive. On the way to
the roses called out in Latin

    behind the sand-traps.
Past the carp fishermen, ramp
    where my ferry ticket turned

to bookmark. On the last day
    of summer, the sun,
a lichen. The fall: punctual.

PRECAMERA

The device I've told you
about, the box of which
you've heard—optical
box, black box, box of
darkness: Dark room. Black room.
The room of days and shadows.
The room in which I work.

TO LEMAÎTRE

When I took him
   for gone
in cuttlefish ink

   he appears
a drawing
   very elegantly framed

and finished
   with his process
but what is his

   process and what is
his paintbrush?
   This Daguerre

DATEBOOK

August 8, 1816

the weather is great the wheat
is ripe in force we reap

how the corn comes along
superb, the peas, potatoes and beans
the hemp equally

through the cut wheat
grew thick green
twists of fate—

the stubble
appears a prairie

August 19, 1839

François Arago officially
the daguerréotype to the Academy
: two centuries ago

an Italian physician pierced a window shutter
with a tiny hole

… alchemy, Wedgwood, chloride

: the indiscretion of a Parisian optician
and Daguerre knew

Niépce, it was certain in 1827,

could shadow shadows
midtone midtones
highlight highlights

when photographically copying engravings
but had given up on reproducing images
from a camera obscura

August 20, 1828

bad weather bemoaned
and slow to obtaining silver plate,
once again declining the use of his burin,
Niépce writes to A.F. Lemaître

I have given up

                                        engravings

I lash my eye
inside *la chambre noire* modified

"My sole object being
to copy Nature with the greatest fidelity"

August 17, 2013

                a honeycomb
I placed on paper
sensitized with iron salts
corrupted it

TO DAGUERRE, 4 JUNE 1827

With this letter
     a plate of pewter

from last spring, cut heliographic

     and a print from the pewter
albeit weak and rich in defects

     (drawing and engraving call me *Stranger*)

oblige me your thoughts and scorn not
     what's possible

were a hand adept at aquatints lent to it

     today I again take up
the countryside bedecked in its emeralds

in which I am fixed
     and solely copying

yes I tried copper
     but more brilliant

do the trees drink from tin

I: When I think of your associates and correspondents it sounds like the beginning of a joke: An inventor, an optician, an engraver and a painter walk into a café …

NN: How do you mean

I: Never mind

NN: I needed lenses, I knew very little about engraving, Daguerre was very good with the "camera," if I may, as well as the effects of light, plus at some point I also needed glasses

I: I wanted to ask about that. How bad is your sight. Can you see me

NN: I can barely hear you

LES VENDANGES, CHARMES

Body moves best
when forgetting

its joints.
Ancients said:

frankincense.
Like Burgundy

I am a land
clouds won't

leave alone.
Body sees best

these rates of
peppered shade.

So a mask
to in darkness

sleep—streetlamp
prevents my mind's

lampblack.
Or vine black,

manufactured
by burning

dried vine stems
packed inside

a pipe. Or bone
black—

char bones,
get a color

that will purify
water.

CONSTITUTIONAL

The city's proposition is a canal
carries to its center as much
the rare barge as it is a terrarium

for clouds and trash gone gossamer
when weather's lottery tumbles up
enough sun to provide contrast

in which such things can be seen.
I propose that when I've talked of
observation, it was to sight I was

giving primacy, a consequence of love
for what my eyes have done to me,
swiveling the mind to what's quick

on the perimeter, then growing calmer
in the yellow angles that end the day.
The canal argues that ducks, too,

have song, even though in my head I see
their sound as action on a chopping block;
and the bread smell blended in gasoline

is a lantern of mysterious yet public
source, a clout the city need not
secrete, for its nature can never be

betrayed; the stones soaked in cold
are known to me, they humidify
my bones during book chapters

and regulate my pace with that of history
when habit would have me rush along.
I've barely bit an apple and air begins

to brown it, but how could I quibble
with hints of snow and lavender
also found within? It is the city's

proposition that I have been less than
fair to the sensorium and have neglected
what full animal I am, data clearly

stating the world far exceeds perception
no matter if it's mind or antennae that
do the receiving. I have been living wrong

while being right enough to get by.
If the numbers adhere to standard fare
I have been about one-third alive.

And now the city feels my body count past
thirty; my knees click like museum guards
when I go to the hardware store in the dark

morning, returning north toward more living
with lag shields, anchors and twine, skin chilled
to accept fresh revelation, bird shit or dye.

Down the canal a barge coughs the black water
white in its wake, and a no-longer-stubborn leaf
twitches in the diesel, which is at this hour just

another name for light I have accepted
with my instruments, instruments whose
weakness includes my only power to change.

NOTICE

Sixty seasons I watched
light composing, decomposing
heaps of it on the

hay, the Saône
an impatient pewter curtain
to keep sky off of fish

In summer, luthier of pears
by autumn it knows
the tunings

This substance the dove
parts on its way
to dark in the dovecote

blanches slate
roofs into isosceles
where once

a cardinal
fell like a blood drop
atop a horse

This discovery I've made
consists of reproducing
these images

NOTES

The images in "Histories" are cameraless cyanotypes I made in 2014 while living in France. The cyanotype process was invented by Sir John Herschel in 1842, so Niépce never used it, but it suited the purposes of this book.

Source material for some of the images:

Pages 14 and 21: Collections of Musée Nicéphore Niépce, Ville de Chalon-Sur-Saône, France, used with the museum's kind permission.

Pages 25 and 27: Collections of Musée Nicéphore Niépce, Ville de Chalon-Sur-Saône, France, used with the museum's kind permission.

Pages 21 and 23: reproduction of a bust of Niépce, created by his son Isidore, which appears as a frontispiece in Victor Fouque, *La verité sur l'invention de la Photographie. Nicéphore Niépce, sa vie, ses essais, ses travaux*, (Chalon-sur-Saône, 1867).

Page 27: ABRACADABRA: Noah Porter, editor, Webster's International Dictionary of the English Language, 1893 (Springfield, G & C. Merriam Company).

I took the photographs in "Les Vendanges" in Chalon-sur-Saône and Saint-Loup-de-Varennes in February 2014.

Works Quoted

Page 16: John Berger, "Why Look at Animals?" in *About Looking* (New York: Knopf Doubleday, 2011), 15.

Page 18: Niépce uses these terms (my translations) in letters to his brother Claude on May 5, 1816 (Collections Musée Nicéphore Niépce, Ville de Chalon-Sur-Saône, France); to A.F. Lemaître on February 16, 1827 (*Dokumentii po istorii izobretenia fotografii*, Leningrad, Academy of Sciences USSR, 1949, 197); and to LJM Daguerre on June 4, 1827 (Fouque, *La Verité*, 136).
Susan Sontag, "The Heroism of Vision" in *On Photography*, (Toronto: McGraw-Hill 1977), 84.

Page 22: Johann Heinrich Schulze's experiments are widely reported in numerous histories of photography, and were originally published in *Scotophorus pro Phosphoro Inventus*, a paper given at the Transactions of the Imperial Academy at Nuremberg in 1719.

W.G. Sebald, *The Rings of Saturn*, trans. Michael Hulse (New York: New Directions, 1998), 182.
Geoffrey Batchen, *Burning With Desire* (Cambridge: The MIT Press, 1991), 101.

Page 22: ibid, 102.
Blaise Cendrars, *Prose du Transsibérien et de la Petite Jeanne De France* (Paris: Éditions Gallimard, 1967), 34.

Page 24: Donna Stonecipher, "Inlay 19 (Jane Jacobs)" in *The Cosmopolitan* (Minneapolis: Coffee House Press, 2008), 74.
Jeffrey and Lisa Smith, "Spending Time on Art," in *Empirical Studies of the Arts*, July 2001 vol. 19 no. 2, 229-236.

Page 26: Henri Cartier-Bresson, *The Mind's Eye*, Writings on Photography and Photographers (New York: Aperture Foundation, 1999), 19.
Christopher James, *The Book of Alternative Photographic Processes*, Second Edition (Clifton Park: Delmar), 2.
Roland Barthes, *Camera Lucida*, trans. Richard Howard (New York: Macmillan 1981), 15.

Page 28: *Dokumentii*, 424-425. This list, which I have excerpted, was compiled and numbered by Niépce and Daguerre in 1829 and 1830, and ultimately reached 101 items during the course of their association. In their correspondence, Niépce and Daguerre protected their research by using only the numbers to refer to the materials.

Page 57: The penultimate line of "Anniversary" is adapted from William Shakespeare's *Hamlet*, Act 4, Scene V.

Page 70: "India for ivory, Sardinia for silver, Attica for honey." Solinus was active in the 3rd century and the author of *Collectanea Rerum Memorabilium* (Collection of Curiosities), from which this quote comes.

Page 77: #6, my imagining of responses received by Niépce from the Bulletin de la Société d'Encouragement pour l'Industrie National; # 9, Fouque, *La verité*, 184.

Page 78: #13, Niépce to Claude, June 16, 1816 (Collections Musée Nicéphore Niépce, Ville de Chalon-sur-Saône, France); #15, Niépce to Vincent Chevalier, December 18, 1828, as quoted in Paul Jay, *Niépce: Genese D'Une Invention* (Chalon-Sur-Saone: Société des Amis du Musée Nicéphore Niépce, 1988), 173.

Page 83: Niépce to A. F. Lemaître, August 20, 1828 (*Dokumentii*, 263).

For a thorough study of the language surrounding the invention of photography, and the desire to photograph, see Geoffrey Batchen's essay "The Naming of Photography: 'A Mass of Metaphor,'" and his book, *Burning With Desire*.

The titles in quotes are various phrases adapted from Niépce's letters (translations mine), as are the italicized lines in "My Heliographic Work Is in Full Swing."

In the poems with titles in italics, I sometimes adapted, collaged, and transformed language from Niépce's letters. What remains of Niépce's correspondence is held at the Musée Nicéphore Niépce in Chalon-sur-Saône, France, and at the Academy of Sciences in Saint Petersburg, Russia. Several volumes of Niépce's letters have been published, primarily in French, including: Victor Fouque, *La verité sur l'invention de la Photographie. Nicéphore Niépce, sa vie, ses essais, ses travaux* (Chalon-sur-Saône: 1867); T.P. Kravetz, editor, *Dokumentii po istorii izobretenia fotografii* (Leningrad: Academy of Sciences USSR, 1949); Paul Jay and E.J. Hobsbawn, editors, *Nicéphore Niépce: Lettres et documents*, Photo Poche edition (Paris: Centre National de la Photographie, 1998); and Manuel Bonnet and Jean-Louis Marignier, editors, *Niépce: Correspondance & Papiers* (Chalon-sur-Saône: Maison Nicéphore Niépce Editions, 2003).

In addition to adapting language from Niépce's letters, and quoting a line from a letter Niépce wrote to A.F. Lemaître on August 20, 1828, the poem "Datebook" adapts text (translations mine) from François Arago's presentation on the daguerreotype, made on August 19, 1839, to the Académie des Sciences de Paris, and originally published in Volume XXXV of *La France littéraire* in 1839.

ACKNOWLEDGMENTS

Grateful acknowledgment is made to the editors of the journals in which the following poems appeared: "Last Visit to Chalon," *The Winter Anthology*, Volume 5, 2015; "Anniversary," *TYPO* 24, 2016.

Thank you to the editors of *Tammy*, who in 2016 published *NN*, a chapbook containing these excerpts and poems: "Can we talk a little about your vocabulary ...'; "It is 1812 ..."; "*February, Jambles*"; "*The Weather, Dear Cousin*"; "Sent by ..."; "You once put a stone in your device ..."; "Mulhouse"; "Tuesday: History of Photography"; "He married ..."; "*À Propos The Motor – 1817*"; "Some say it was the motor ..."; "Les Vendanges, Charmes"; "He Was Joseph, First"; "*The Experiments – To Claude, 1817*"; "It cannot be corroborated..."; "*Your Packet, Dear Cousin*"; "*The Experiments – Spring 1817*"; "You had some success with glass ... "; "Mont Avril"; "Born on March 7, 1765 ..."; "*The Experiments*"; "*To Claude*"; "The point de vue d'après nature ..."; "Short Biographies" ; "Last Visit to Chalon"; "*Notice*"

This book would not have been possible without a grant from the United States Fulbright Program, nor without the help of staff at the Musée Nicéphore Niépce, especially Émilie Bernard and Christian Passeri. Thank you.

Profound gratitude to the many teachers, friends, colleagues and individuals who assisted directly or indirectly in the making of this book, and who are too numerous to name here. Thank you Timothy Donnelly and Dan Leers. Special thanks to Carey McHugh and Robert Ostrom for their comments on this manuscript; to my parents, for their continued love and support; and to Sofia Verzbolovskis, for constant love and adventure.

I am also grateful to Calvin Bedient for selecting this manuscript, and to Gillian Hamel, Ken Keegan, Rusty Morrison, Cassandra Smith, and all the staff at Omnidawn for their work in realizing this book.

photo by Sofia Verzbolovskis

Andrew Seguin is a poet and photographer who was born in Pittsburgh in 1981. He is the author of two chapbooks, *Black Anecdote* and *NN*, and his poems have appeared widely in literary journals, including *A Public Space*, *Boston Review*, *Gulf Coast* and *Iowa Review*. His work often explores the intersection of language and image, and has been supported by the Fulbright Program, the Pennsylvania Humanities Council, and Poets House. Andrew lives in New York City.

The Room In Which I Work
by Andrew Seguin

Cover Art: Andrew Seguin, Untitled, Cyanotype, 2014
All images in Histories: Andrew Seguin, Untitled Cyanotypes, 2014
All photographs in Les Vendanges are by Andrew Seguin:
p. 72: Saint-Loup-de-Varennes, 2014
p. 73: Rue de l'Oratoire, 2014
p. 74: Le Gras, 2014

Cover and interior typefaces: Adobe Jenson Pro & Perpetua Std
Cover and interior design by Cassandra Smith

Offset printed in the United States
by Edwards Brothers Malloy, Ann Arbor, Michigan
On 55# Glatfelter B18 Antique
Acid Free Archival Quality Recycled Paper

Publication of this book was made possible in part by gifts from:
The New Place Fund
Robin & Curt Caton

Omnidawn Publishing
Oakland, California
2017

Rusty Morrison & Ken Keegan, senior editors & co-publishers
Gillian Olivia Blythe Hamel, managing editor
Cassandra Smith, poetry editor & book designer
Sharon Zetter, poetry editor, book designer & development officer
Liza Flum, poetry editor & marketing assistant
Peter Burghardt, poetry editor
Juliana Paslay, fiction editor
Gail Aronson, fiction editor
Cameron Stuart, marketing assistant
Avren Keating, administrative assistant
Kevin Peters, *OmniVerse* Lit Scene editor
Sara Burant, *OmniVerse* reviews editor
Josie Gallup, publicity assistant
SD Sumner, copyeditor
Briana Swain, marketing assistant